Jam Session

Lisa Leslie

Terri Dougherty
ABDO Publishing Company

visit us at
www.abdopub.com

Published by ABDO Publishing Company, 4940 Viking Drive, Suite 622, Edina, Minnesota 55435.
Copyright © 1999 by Abdo Consulting Group, Inc. International copyrights reserved in all countries.
No part of this book may be reproduced in any form without written permission from the publisher.

Printed in the United States.

Cover and Interior Photo credits: AP/Wide World Photos

Edited by Denis Dougherty

Sources: Knight-Ridder News; Los Angeles Times; NBA Inside Stuff; New York Dailey News;
People Magazine; Sports Illustrated; Sports Illustrated For Kids; USA Today

Library of Congress Cataloging-in-Publication Data

Dougherty, Terri.
    Lisa Leslie / Terri Dougherty.
        p. cm. -- (Jam Session)
    Includes index.
    Summary: Describes the life and career of the player who led the 1996 women's Olympic
    basketball team to win the gold medal for the United States in Atlanta
    ISBN 1-57765-313-0 (hardcover)
    ISBN 1-57765-345-9 (paperback)
    1. Leslie, Lisa, 1972- --Juvenile literature. 2. Basketball players--United States--
    Biography--Juvenile literature. 3. Women basketball players -- United States -- Biography --
    Juvenile literature. [1. Leslie, Lisa, 1972- . 2. Basketball players. 3. Women -- Biography.
    4. Afro-Americans--Biography.] I. Title. II. Series.
    GV884.L47D68 1999
    796.323'64'092--dc21
    [B]

                                                                        98-27129
                                                                            CIP
                                                                             AC

Contents

A Model Player

Lisa Leslie is as comfortable in a fancy evening gown as she is in tennis shoes. She can walk gracefully down a runway in a fashion show, or run full blast down a basketball court to score on a fast break.

Lisa is a professional basketball player in the WNBA. Lisa is also a model. She doesn't see anything odd about her career combination.

Lisa Leslie goes in for the layup in front of Sacramento Monarchs' Tajama Abraham.

"Whether I'm on the court or on the runway, I'm out there entertaining," Lisa said. "They're the same for me." Lisa played on the women's basketball team that won a gold medal in the 1996 Olympics. That summer, she signed a contract with a big modeling agency. After the Olympics, she also signed a contract to play in the WNBA.

"I'm passionate about both, and when I'm doing both, I'm giving you me," she said. "I'm being aggressive, doing what I love and what I've practiced with attitude and style. The big difference is, I'm showered and clean when I'm modeling. The point is, I am a woman, always."

Opponents have to watch out when Lisa takes off her fancy dress and puts on her basketball uniform. "When I put on those shorts, forget it. Don't mess with my teammates. Don't mess with me," Lisa said. "It's kind of a zone. They say you get into a zone when you shoot. I get into a zone when I change clothes."

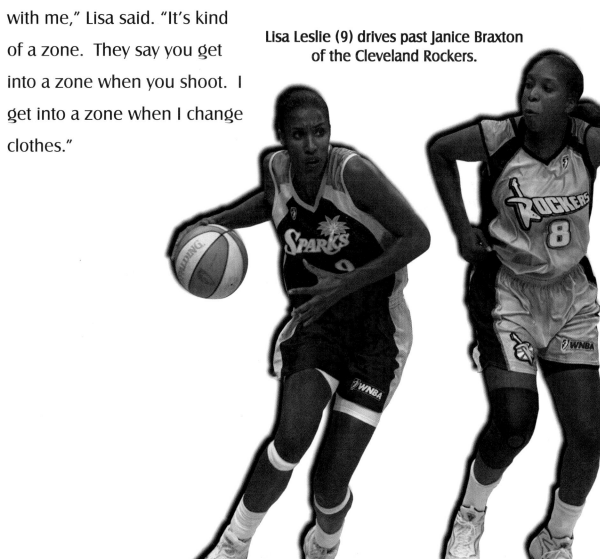

Lisa Leslie (9) drives past Janice Braxton of the Cleveland Rockers.

Head and Shoulders Above the Rest

*L*isa didn't always love basketball. She was very tall in grade school and grew tired of people asking her if she played basketball. "I got so sick of everyone asking me," Lisa remembers. "I developed this real bad attitude toward sports, especially basketball."

Lisa was six feet tall when she was in second grade, a head taller than her teacher! Other kids in school weren't kind about her height. They laughed at her and called her names.

The teasing was even more difficult for Lisa because her mother was away from home for long periods of time. When Lisa was in grade school, her mother, Christine Leslie-Espinoza, bought an 18-wheel semi-truck and drove across the country to support Lisa and her two sisters. The girls stayed with relatives or friends while their mother was gone. "There were some sad times," Lisa said. "Mom had to travel so far and so long. But we understood she had to do it. It made me mature really fast. I had so much to do."

Lisa's mom could only visit her daughters once or twice a month between 1982 and 1985 when she was driving across the country.

"I cried all day wishing my mom was home," Lisa said.

But when Christine came home, she reassured Lisa that things would turn out fine. Christine was 6-foot-3, and told Lisa that she had been picked on, too. But that hadn't stopped her from doing a tough job, and still looking like a woman. "The closer I got to my mother's height," Lisa said, "the more beautiful I felt."

Lisa would pretend she was a model. She would put books on top of her head and walk around her house. This helped her learn to walk smoothly. She also practiced signing her name so she would be ready to sign autographs when she became famous.

Lisa admired her mom and the hard work she did. Her mom was her role model. "My mom taught me the importance of responsibility and hard work," Lisa said.

Sometimes during summer vacation, Lisa and her younger sister, Tiffany, got to ride along with their mom in the truck. They would sleep on a bunk in the back of the truck. "It was 36 inches (91cm) wide," Lisa's mom remembers. "All of us would jam in there. We had to hold on to each other. That helps us now. We all hold on to each other in a lot of ways."

Basketball Beginnings

Lisa's attitude toward basketball changed when she was in seventh grade. Her friend Sharon Hargrove encouraged her to play on the basketball team.

Lisa listened to Sharon, who was class president and later went on to play college basketball at the University of Nevada-Las Vegas. But Lisa thought, "If I fall down, I'm quitting."

Lisa may have fallen down, but she didn't quit. And she's happy she stuck with basketball. "I always wonder what would have happened to me if I hadn't picked up that ball," Lisa said. "I don't know. Basketball's done a lot for me. Put me through college and let me go around the world. It's done wonders for me."

On the basketball court, Lisa didn't have many women to pattern herself after. So she closely watched men's basketball players. "There weren't that many [female] role models, at least not many that I knew of," Lisa said. "If, by the way I play, I can be a role model or encourage someone else, that would be wonderful."

Lisa Leslie shoots the ball at
the University of Southern
California in 1993.

Pouring in the Points

By ninth grade, Lisa had improved her game. She was 6-foot-3, and could dunk the ball! She attended Morningside High School in Inglewood, California, and her team won the state championship during her junior year.

She was recognized as the best high school player in the nation, and was the star of the United States Olympic junior national team that toured Spain. Lisa was also a good student. She was class president three of her four years at Morningside, and had a 3.5 grade point average.

Toward the end of her senior year, Lisa accomplished a feat that put her in basketball history books. She wanted to break the record for most points scored in a single game.

Cheryl Miller, generally considered the best women's player ever, had once scored 105 points in a high school game. On February 7, 1990, Lisa wanted to break that record.

She planned to score 25 or 30 points each quarter. But the shots fell more easily than she could have imagined. She couldn't believe how many points she quickly scored.

"I heard a buzzer and looked up at the scoreboard," Lisa remembers. "It showed us up 49-6. I asked, 'Is this the half?' " No, it was only the end of the first quarter! At half time, Morningside was ahead of South Torrace 102-24. Lisa had scored all but one of her team's points.

But South Torrace didn't like getting beat badly just so Lisa could break the record. One of the team's players was injured in the first half, and another two fouled out. This left South Torrace with only four healthy players to start the second half. The team's coach decided to forfeit the game. The game ended with Lisa four points shy of the record.

Lisa did set a record for most free throws made in a game, converting 27 of 35 shots from the line. She also converted on 37 of 56 field-goal attempts. "It wasn't personal," Lisa said. "They knew I was going for the record. I thought knowing that would take some of the hurt away."

That year, Lisa averaged 27.3 points, 15.1 rebounds, three assists and seven blocked shots per game. She won the Dial Award, given annually to the nation's outstanding high school scholar-athlete.

"If I'd let her, she could have averaged 50 points a game instead of 27," Morningside coach Frank Scott said.

Another Star at Southern Cal

*W*hen Lisa started college at the University of Southern California, she was compared to former USC superstar Cheryl Miller, whose record she had almost broken.

"Lisa has the potential to be as dominant as Cheryl," Washington coach Chris Gobrecht said.

Lisa believed she could do it. "I don't want this to sound like I'm cocky or anything," Lisa said. "But by the time I get to my senior year, I think I can be just as good as Cheryl."

Lisa recognized that she could help make women's basketball more popular. "I think we do need that one star that even people who aren't that familiar with the game can recognize," Lisa said. "It not only gets the attention of the public, it gets the attention of the kids who will grow up to be the next superstars. The next Cheryl Miller, whoever she is, can have an impact on women's basketball for years after her career is over."

Lisa also had a lot to learn. As a freshman, she averaged 19.4 points, 10 rebounds, and 2.6 blocked shots per game. She was voted the Pac-10 Freshman of the Year. But she also committed almost four fouls per game, and fouled out nine times.

Lisa goes for a layup while
playing for USC.

"I think it was a revelation to Lisa that there were weaknesses in her game that other people could exploit," USC coach Marianne Stanley said. "There's a lot that she's still learning. She's like the colt who wants to get up and go and isn't real secure with all the skills yet."

During her college career, Lisa was named an All-American three times. She won the national Player of the Year award in 1994, her senior year. She led the Trojans to four NCAA Tournament appearances, and set Pac-10 records for scoring with 2,414 points and blocks with 321.

"A lot of coaches have said I have the potential to be the kind of player who can help women's basketball reach more people," Lisa said. "I guess you never know when you've fulfilled those expectations. All I can do is try to be the kind of player my team needs, and if that's what women's basketball as a whole needs—great!"

But when Lisa graduated, there were no professional leagues for women in the United States. "I think we are cheated as a gender," Lisa said. "No one knows what happens to all the great people in our game. It seems like we're written off."

Lisa Leslie takes the ball
down the court for USC.

Hoops and High Heels

With no pro women's league in the U.S., Lisa went to play basketball in Europe. She spent 1995 playing for Sicilgesso in Alcemo, Italy. She averaged 23 points and 12 rebounds a game.

Then she heard that women's professional basketball leagues were being formed in the United States. She was excited about playing in her own country.

"All I gave up was playing in somebody else's country, eating somebody else's food, and trying to understand somebody else's language," Lisa said.

But Lisa also had another career to consider: modeling. During the summer of 1996, she signed a modeling contract with Wilhemina Models in New York. "Now I can answer all the people in the shopping malls that, yes, I am a model," Lisa said.

Lisa wanted to show girls and women that they could be feminine as well as athletic, and that they had many career opportunities to choose from.

"We have to stop feeling that we've got to choose one thing and cut off our other options," Lisa said. "You can be whatever you want to be. Women don't have to fulfill the stereotype of looking like men with their clothes hanging off them just because they play basketball."

Lisa appeared in *Vogue* and *TV Guide* that summer, and was friendly to the other models.

"I talk to everybody. And I won't even take that dumb model treatment. I'm very intelligent, and I know it," Lisa said. "I'm going to go into the modeling world and break through barriers."

Her basketball playing even enhanced her modeling career. "Most of the companies that hire me like my athletic look," Lisa adds.

As Good as Gold

*A*fter Lisa left her team in Italy, she began playing for the USA Basketball National Team that went on to win a gold medal in the 1996 Summer Olympics.

To prepare for the Olympics, the team toured the world for nine months, playing in nine countries.

Lisa Leslie takes the ball to the hoop against Cuba's Judith Aguila during one of the USA's 52 exhibition games.

The U.S. played 52 games and won every one. Lisa, who is 6-foot-5, was the team's top scorer and second-leading rebounder.

Then it was on to Atlanta for the Olympics. The opening ceremonies did not go smoothly for Lisa, who slipped out of a high heel while walking down a ramp!

"I had to grab (men's basketball star) Karl Malone to get my shoe back on," Lisa said.

The U.S. women's basketball team breezed through the early rounds. The team's 93-71 win over Australia in a semifinal game put them in the gold-medal game.

Lisa scored 22 points and grabbed 13 rebounds in front of 31,854 fans in the semifinal at the Georgia Dome. Still, she didn't take anything for granted.

"It's kind of like we're relieved we've made it this far," Lisa said.

Lisa Leslie is pumped up during the gold medal women's basketball game.

The United States faced Brazil for the gold medal. Brazil had beaten the U.S. in the 1994 World Championships. Most of the same players were again facing each other for Olympic gold.

"The last time we played Brazil they left a sour taste in our mouths,"

Lisa said. "I visualized after the game playing them again. I don't think there's a better time to play them. I look forward to the challenge. We know how to win."

At halftime the Americans led by 11. But coach Tara VanDerveer remembered the U.S. had a 20-point lead over Brazil in the World Championships, and had lost the game. "I don't think anyone felt comfortable at halftime," the coach said.

At the start of the second half, the United States showed it wasn't going to let the lead slip away again. Sheryl Swoopes and Katrina McClain scored on fast breaks, and McClain scored off an inbounds pass. Then it was Lisa's turn. She blocked a shot and scored off a pass from Theresa Edwards. The U.S. led 65-46!

Lisa made 12 of 14 field-goal attempts, an incredible 86

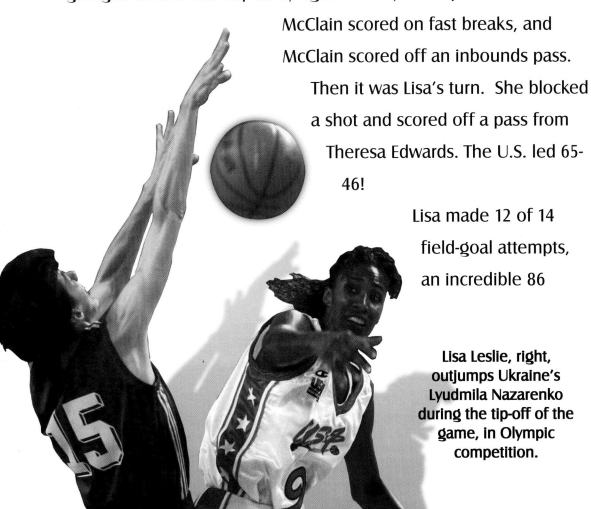

Lisa Leslie, right, outjumps Ukraine's Lyudmila Nazarenko during the tip-off of the game, in Olympic competition.

percent in a pressure-packed game. Several of her baskets came on jump shots from a dozen feet out. She also made five free throws for a total of 29 points. The United States won 111-87!

"Considering this was the gold-medal game, I'd say our team played its best," Lisa said. "It was just very emotional for me."

Lisa Leslie, center, cries before receiving the gold medal in women's Olympic basketball.

Starring Role in the WNBA

"**A**m I excited?" Lisa asked as the WNBA's first season was about to begin. "I'm excited and I'm ready." Lisa was about to begin her U.S. professional basketball career as a member of the Los Angeles Sparks. She had stayed busy before the season started, doing some sports reporting for NBC and TNT. And she also continued her modeling career.

"That's what I call my Wonder Woman Theory," Lisa said. "When I'm playing, I'll sweat and talk trash. However, off the court I'm lipstick, heels, and short skirts. I'm very feminine, mild-mannered, and sensitive. Men have been allowed to be individuals and play a team sport. Now we can be seen as individuals too. We can have personalities."

Lisa was proud to be in the WNBA. The license plates on her white Mercedes-Benz S500 read LLWNBA. "The intensity among the women may be greater [than in men's or college games] from start to finish," Lisa said. "If you watch you'll see the quickness and the talent."

Lisa's quickness and determination looked to make her a star in the new league. "Lisa has an incredible drive to win," her friend Shaquille O'Neal, a star with the NBA's Los Angeles Lakers, said. "She hates to lose, even during a pickup game."

Lisa was named her team's captain, and quickly proved she was worthy of the title. She led the league in rebounding with 9.5 per game. She led the Sparks in scoring at 15.9 points per game, and was third in the league in scoring and second in blocks. She was named to the 1997 All-WNBA First Team.

"When it's time to play, something clicks in my mind, and I become—it's almost like a monster," Lisa said. "My favorite phrase is, 'Let's go for the jugular.'"

Lisa Leslie, Rebecca Lobo, and Sheryl Swoopes have starring roles in the WNBA.

A Bright Future

Lisa continues to be a dominant player for the Sparks, who finished their first season in the WNBA with a 14-14 record, second in the Western Conference.

"Lisa's dominating and physical and then, after the game is over, she transforms into this stunning woman," former Lakers star James Worthy said. "She brings an added dimension to the game, the same way Michael Jordan does."

Director Spike Lee, left, keeps a watchful eye on Lisa Leslie, center, and Dawn Staley, right, on the set of the Nike commercial for women's shoes.

When her basketball and modeling careers are over, Lisa may turn to acting and broadcasting. She has already appeared in the TV shows "Hangtime", "Moesha", and "Sister Sister", and has done sideline reporting for "NBA on TNT" and "NBA's Inside Stuff." She would love to "make it to the big screen" and "play the role of a super hero."

Lisa's goal in basketball is to be an all-around player like one of her favorites, Hakeem Olajuwon of the Houston Rockets. She's also happy to be making her mark as an all-around woman.

"I like that I can help change people's perspectives about what women can and can't do," Lisa said. "When I am finished playing, I hope people will remember me as the most versatile center to ever play the game, man or woman."

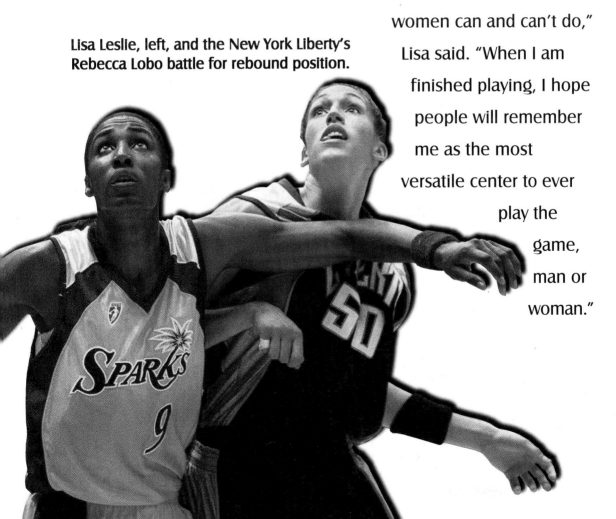

Lisa Leslie, left, and the New York Liberty's Rebecca Lobo battle for rebound position.

Lisa DeShaun Leslie - Profile

Born: July 7, 1972

Hometown: Gardena, California

High School: Morningside High School in Inglewood, California

College: University of Southern California

Professional Team: Los Angeles Sparks

Position: Center

Height: 6 feet, 5 inches

Weight: 170 lbs.

Personal: Lisa's favorite NBA team is the Los Angeles Lakers, and former Lakers star James Worthy was her favorite player. Her favorite athlete is track and field star Jackie Joyner-Kersee. She likes to play board games and cards, and listens to rap music if she's exercising and gospel when she's relaxing. Her favorite movie is *Pretty Woman.* The woman she admires most is her mom, Christine Leslie-Espinoza.

Awards and Honors

USA Today Prep Player of the Year (1990)

All Pac-10 First Team (1991, 1992, 1993, 1994)

Pac-10 Freshman of the Year (1991)

USA Basketball Player of the Year (1993)

National Player of the Year (1994)

Olympic gold medalist (1996)

All-WNBA First Team (1997)

**Los Angeles Sparks
center Lisa Leslie.**

Chronology

1972 - Born on July 7 in Gardena, California.

1989 - Member of the U.S. team in the Junior World Championships.

1990 - Scored 101 points in the first half of a high school basketball game. The opponent forfeited the game at halftime.

  - Began college at the University of Southern California.

1991 - Named to the All-Pac 10 First Team.

  - Member of the U.S. World University Games team.

1992 - Named to the All-Pac 10 First Team.

1993 - Selected as USA Basketball Player of the Year.

  - Named to the All-Pac 10 First Team

1994 - Named to the All-Pac 10 First Team.

  - Member of the U.S. Goodwill Games team.

  - Member of the U.S. World Championship team.

  - Naismith Award winner, given to the nation's top player.

  - National Player of the Year.

1995 - Played basketball for Sicilgesso, in Italy, averaging 23 points and 12 rebounds per game.

  - Joined the USA Basketball Women's National Team.

1996 - Signed contract with Wilhemina Models, Inc.

- Member of USA Women's Olympic Team. Won gold medal, led team in scoring (19.5 ppg).

1997 - Named to All-WNBA First Team.

- Led Los Angeles Sparks in scoring (15.9 ppg) and led WNBA in rebounds (9.5 rpg).

- Member of the WNBA European Touring Team.

- Completed degree in communications at USC.

1998 - Member of the U.S. Women's World Championship team.

Lisa Leslie (9) out rebounds the Houston Comets' Tina Thompson (7), Cynthia Cooper (14), and Janeth Arcain.

Glossary

BLOCKED SHOT - A defensive player knocking away an offensive player's shot attempt.

CAPTAIN - A team member designated as the team's leader.

DUNK - To slam the ball through the basket.

FAST BREAK - To move the ball quickly down the court in an attempt to score before the opponent can set up its defense.

FOUL OUT - To commit more than the allowable number of fouls in a game and have to leave the game.

Lisa Leslie is a fan-favorite in Los Angeles and around the world.

FRESHMAN - A student in the first year of high school or college in the United States.

GOLD MEDAL - Prize given to the top team in certain competitions, such as the Olympics.

HALFTIME - Rest period between the first half and the second half of a basketball game.

NCAA - National Collegiate Athletic Association. The governing body for college sports.

PROFESSIONAL - To earn one's living from an activity or sport.

REBOUND - To grab the ball after a missed shot.

WNBA - Women's National Basketball Association. A professional league for women's basketball players.

Lisa grabs a rebound as Dena Head, of the Utah Starzz, looks on.

Index